Decomposers

Greg Roza

The Rosen Publishing Group's
PowerKids Press™
New York

Published in 2009 by The Rosen Publishing Group, Inc.
29 East 21st Street, New York, NY 10010

Book Design: Michael J. Flynn

Photo Credits: Cover © Peter Anderson/Dorling Kindersley/Getty Images; pp. 4–29 (dirt border) © mates/Shutterstock; p. 4 (deer) © Kim Worrell/Shutterstock; p. 5 (bear) © Oksana Perkins/Shutterstock; p. 6 (bear) © letty17/Shutterstock; p. 6 (grass) © Travis Houston/Shutterstock; p. 6 (tree) © Jan Martin Will/Shutterstock; p. 6 (squirrel) © Eric Isselée/Shutterstock; p. 6 (sun) © Alfgar/Shutterstock; p. 6 (deer) © James Pierce/Shutterstock; p. 6 (mountain lion) © Ultrashock/Shutterstock; p. 8 (leaf) © Vladimir/Shutterstock; p. 9 (forest) © majeczka/Shutterstock; p. 10 (woman eating apple) © Mango Productions/Corbis; pp. 10–11 (woman jogging) © Gunta Klavina/Shutterstock; p. 12 (hyena) © J. Norman Reid/Shutterstock; p. 12 (vulture) © Jan Coetzee/Shutterstock; p. 13 (dung beetle) © Johann Hayman/Shutterstock; p. 14 (earthworms) © mashe/Shutterstock; p. 14 (worm casts) © Robert Pickett/Corbis; p. 15 (Darwin) © PoodlesRock/Corbis; p. 16 (tablespoon of dirt) © marekuliasz/Shutterstock; p. 17 (bacteria) © Charles O'Rear/Corbis; p. 19 (bacteria) © David Scharf/Science Faction/Getty Images; p. 20 (peas) © Yellowj/Shutterstock; pp. 21 (rhizobium nodules), 27 (turtle) © Visuals Unlimited/Corbis; p. 22 (mushrooms) © fotosav/Shutterstock; p. 23 (top) © Arkadiusz Stachowski/Shutterstock; p. 23 (bottom) © Patricia Hofmeester/Shutterstock; p. 25 (moldy strawberry) © Ed Phillips/Shutterstock; p. 28 (first compost) © Sharon Day/Shutterstock; p. 28 (second compost) © Peter Clark/Shutterstock; p. 28 (third compost) © Barbro Bergfeldt/Shutterstock; p. 29 (compost) © Joan Ramon Menndo Escoda/Shutterstock.

Library of Congress Cataloging-in-Publication Data

Roza, Greg.
    Decomposers / Greg Roza.
        p. cm. — (Real life readers)
    Includes index.
    ISBN: 978-1-4358-0145-5
    6-pack ISBN: 978-1-4358-0146-2
    ISBN 978-1-4358-2981-7 (library binding)
    1. Biodegradation—Juvenile literature. I. Title.
    QH530.5.R69 2009
    577'.16—dc22
                                                2008038427

Manufactured in the United States of America

Contents

Caught in the Food Web

All living things need food to **survive**. Their bodies break down the food into the **nutrients** they need to live and grow. An adult person needs to eat three to six meals a day, depending on the person and the size of the meals. Some animals eat far more than a person does. An elephant, for example, may eat over 700 pounds (318 kg) of food a day! Plants also need food to survive, but they make their own.

In our homes, we water our plants and feed our animals every day. Without our help, they might not survive. In the wild, however, plants and animals need to care for themselves. Wild plants and animals live in one of Earth's many **ecosystems**. Each **organism** in an ecosystem is part of a food web.

A food web is an arrangement of feeding relationships between the organisms found in an ecosystem.

Food webs start with plants. Plants are known as producers because they use sunlight, **carbon dioxide**, water, and nutrients from the soil to make, or produce, food for themselves. The nutrients plants se for growth are stored inside their **tissues** as they grow larger.

Animals are called consumers because they eat, or consume, plants or other animals. A consumer's body **digests** the plants or animals it eats and takes in the nutrients that were trapped in their tissues. Animals that get the nutrients they need by eating only plants—such as the deer shown on page 4—are called herbivores (UHR-buh-vohrz). Those that get nutrients by eating other animals are called carnivores (KAHR-nuh-vohrz). Some animals get nutrients by eating both plants and animals. They're called omnivores (AHM-nih-vohrz).

Together, producers and consumers form food webs . . . well, almost. You might be wondering how

Brown bears are omnivores. In addition to fish, they also eat rodents, nuts, berries, leaves, and roots.

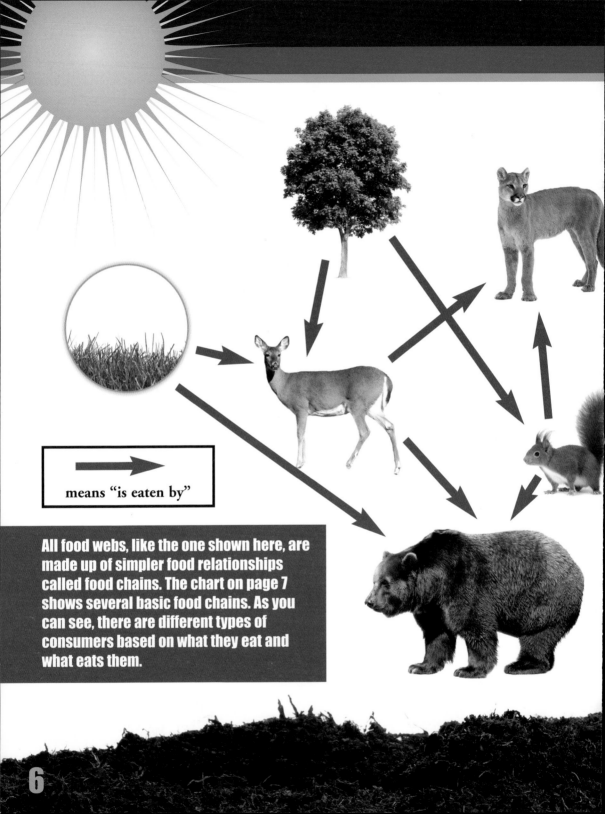

means "is eaten by"

All food webs, like the one shown here, are made up of simpler food relationships called food chains. The chart on page 7 shows several basic food chains. As you can see, there are different types of consumers based on what they eat and what eats them.

he nutrients locked in the tissues of the largest consumers—such as lions, sharks, and even people—are released back into the ecosystem for producers to use once again. The answer is decomposition.

Food Chains

	forest	grassland	ocean
producer (plant)	leaf	grass	seaweed
primary, or first-level, consumer (herbivore)	caterpillar	mouse	fish
secondary, or second-level, consumer (carnivore or omnivore)	robin	snake	seal
tertiary, or third-level, consumer (carnivore or omnivore)	owl	hawk	shark

What Is Decomposition?

Have you ever heard the word "composition"? It's the process of combining small parts to form a larger whole. A composer, for example, is a musician who combines notes and words to make a song. In nature, you might say that plants and animals are composers. The bodies of living things combine the nutrients in the foods they digest to form new tissue (or grow) and to create energy.

Decomposition is the opposite of composition. It's the process of breaking things down into smaller parts. In nature, dead organisms rot, which means they slowly break down into the basic nutrients other organisms need for growth and energy. For example, in many areas of the world, leaves turn brown in autumn and fall to the ground. Over time, weather and other natural forces slowly break the leaves down until their parts are small enough to mix in with the soil.

Leaves on a forest floor rot and release nutrients back into the soil. Trees use the nutrients to grow new leaves.

What Is a Decomposer?

If autumn leaves and other dead **organic** matter were left to themselves to decompose, the process could take a very long time. Dead organisms would pile up all over the world. Nutrients would remain trapped in this dead matter, making it harder for living plants and animals to get them. Fortunately, decomposers make this process quicker. A decomposer is an organism that eats

When you think about it, even people are like decomposers! We eat plants and animals that were recently alive and our bodies break them down into smaller pieces that we use for growth and energy. However, we can't return nutrients to the soil and air like real decomposers can.

dead organisms to get the nutrients it needs for energy and growth. It also leaves behind nutrients for other living things. Another word for decomposer is "saprotroph" (SAA-pruh-trohf), which comes from the ancient Greek words for "rotten" and "food."

Decomposition may sound gross, but it's a natural process that's necessary for the survival of life on Earth. If decomposers didn't do their job, it would take a long time for organisms to break down after they died. Nutrients, particularly carbon and **nitrogen**, would remain trapped in dead plants and animals for a very long time. Plants wouldn't be able to get the nutrients they need for growth. Animals that eat plants wouldn't get the nutrients they need. Without decomposers, food webs would fall apart, and life on Earth as we know it wouldn't be possible.

Break It Down

vulture

Decomposition often begins with scavengers. Many scavengers—such as vultures, crows, and hyenas—are consumers that often feed on **carrion** instead of hunting for their food. They are sometimes considered one of the first decomposers to feed on dead organisms and break them down into smaller pieces.

hyena

Detritivores

Detritivores (dih-TRY-tuh-vohrz)—or detritus (dih-TRY-tuhs) feeders—are small scavengers. "Detritus" is a word describing nonliving organic matter. Another word for it is "garbage." Detritivores help break down organic matter

Some female dung beetles roll animal dung, or solid animal waste, into a ball and lay their eggs in it. When the eggs hatch, the young beetles get the nutrients they need for growth by eating the dung.

into smaller pieces, making it easier for other decomposers to do their job. Detritivores often eat smaller decomposers that have already begun to feed off detritus. Some detritivores—such as the dung beetle—feed on solid animal waste. The solid waste of herbivores often contains large amounts of undigested plant matter, which makes a great meal for a dung beetle!

Earthworms are important detritivores. They feed mainly on dead plants, breaking them down into smaller parts. Earthworms may eat dead plants in the soil, or they may drag dead leaves underground to feed on. Earthworms leave

Earthworms are a sign of healthy soil. One acre (0.4 ha) of healthy soil may be home to a million earthworms!

behind small piles of nutrient-rich solid waste, called casts, that help support plant life.

Common insect detritivores include termites, wood lice, millipedes, cockroaches, and some kinds of beetles. Many insects—such as flies—lay their eggs on dead animals. When the eggs hatch, the **larvae** begin to feed on the dead animal. This gives them the nutrients and energy they need for growth.

Other detritivores include slugs, snails, and fiddler crabs. Scavengers and

worm casts

detritivores help break down dead organic matter, but they always leave behind a lot of unused nutrients. Finishing decomposition is the responsibility of even smaller decomposers—many so small we can't see them without special tools.

Charles Darwin and the Earthworm

Charles Darwin was an English naturalist (a scientist who studies plants and animals). In 1881, after years of studying earthworms, Darwin wrote this about them: "It may be doubted whether there are many other animals which have played so important a part in the history of the world as have these lowly organized creatures." Darwin discovered that earthworms play an important role in preparing the soil to support plant life. Earthworms make tunnels in the soil, which allows air and water to reach plant roots and other tiny creatures living in the soil. They also help break down dead plants, unlocking nutrients important for all life on Earth.

Bacteria

Bacteria are one-celled organisms that live almost everywhere on Earth. They're so small we need a microscope to see them. Some cause illness, but many are helpful. Bacteria are the primary, or main, decomposers of carrion. They're also the primary decomposers of dead plants in some ecosystems.

You might wonder how something so small could be responsible for most of the decomposition in the world. It's because they're so plentiful. A single tablespoon of soil contains billions of bacteria! Bacteria **reproduce** very quickly to form huge colonies. The colonies of some bacteria types can double in size in just 20 minutes. Only a lack of food causes the colony to grow smaller as bacteria die.

How Do Bacteria Eat?

Bacteria make **enzymes** they put into the organic matter around them. The enzymes break down the matter into nutrients small enough to pass

hrough the cell walls of bacteria. Bacteria take in some of these nutrients to make energy. The rest usually get mixed into the soil where they're used by plants and other organisms. Bacteria also give off several gases when breaking own matter. They put carbon back into the ecosystem in the form of carbon

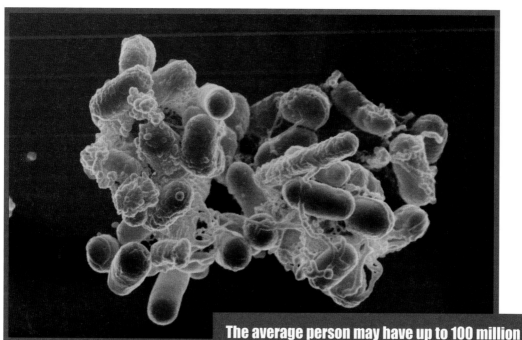

The average person may have up to 100 million bacteria inside them! Bacteria in our digestive system help us digest things we normally couldn't digest. They also kill harmful bacteria.

dioxide—a gas plants need to make food. Other gases are the reason organic matter smells so bad when it rots.

Tough Work

One very important group of bacterial decomposers are the actinomycete (ak-tih-noh-MY-seets). They live in the soil and help break down tough plant tissues other organisms can't digest. By breaking down bark, **chitin**, and even newspaper, they make these materials easier for other bacteria to digest.

An actinomycete colony forms long, thin threads as it spreads out in the soil. It looks a little like a spider web. The earthy smell of soil comes from actinomycetes.

Bacteria and the Nitrogen Cycle

Nitrogen is a gas that plants and animals need to live. The air we breathe is mostly nitrogen, but most plants and animals can't take it in from the air.

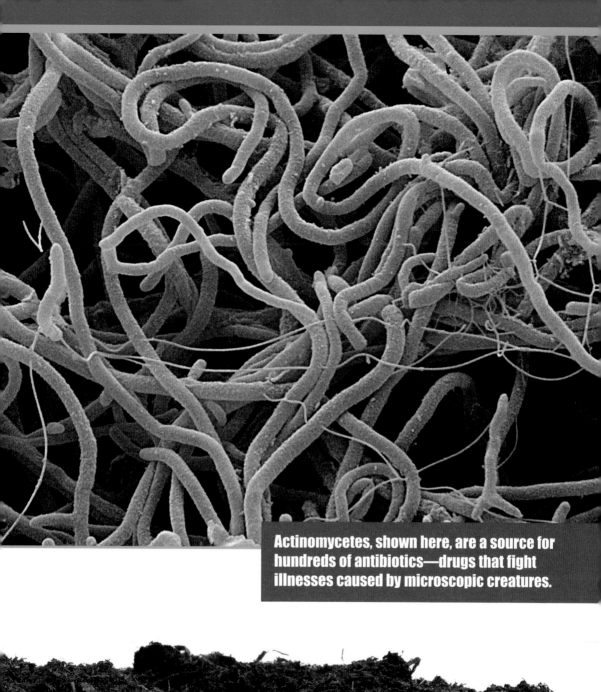

Actinomycetes, shown here, are a source for hundreds of antibiotics—drugs that fight illnesses caused by microscopic creatures.

Thanks to several kinds of bacteria, plants and animals are able to get the nitrogen they need to live.

Bacteria called rhizobia (ry-ZOH-bee-uh) live on the roots of legumes (such as beans, peanuts, and peas). They change nitrogen in the air into nitrogen compounds plants can use. The plants use the nitrogen compounds to make **protein**, which they need to build new cells. In return, the bacteria receive nutrients they need for growth from the plants. A large portion of the nitrogen compounds created by rhizobia remains in the soil for other plants to use. This is just one example of how bacteria help bring nitrogen to plants.

All animals need nitrogen to make protein. Consumers get much of the nitrogen they need by eating plants like legumes. When dead plants and animals decompose, nitrogen is just one of the many nutrients that are recycled back into the environment. Furthermore, some kinds of bacteria put nitrogen back into the air. These are all steps in the nitrogen cycle.

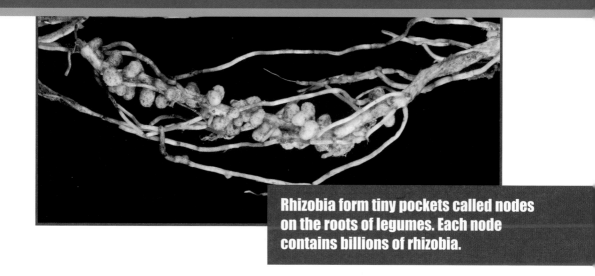

Rhizobia form tiny pockets called nodes on the roots of legumes. Each node contains billions of rhizobia.

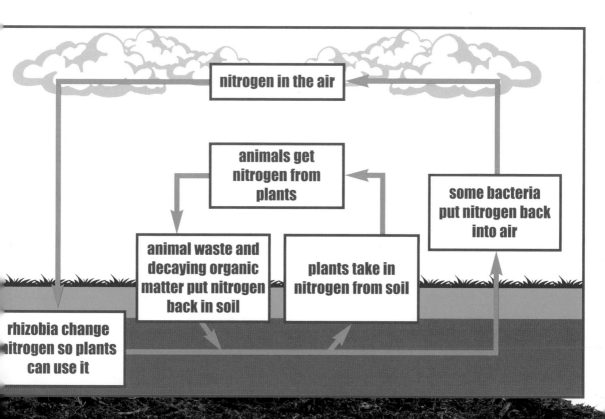

nitrogen in the air

animals get nitrogen from plants

some bacteria put nitrogen back into air

animal waste and decaying organic matter put nitrogen back in soil

plants take in nitrogen from soil

rhizobia change nitrogen so plants can use it

Fungi

Just like bacteria, fungi (the plural form of "fungus") are found in many forms all over the world. There are more than 70,000 kinds of fungi! You're probably most familiar with the fungi we call mushrooms and toadstools, but fungi also include mold, mildew, yeast, and many others. Fungi aren't plants, although many people think they are because they often grow on or in the soil. They don't make their own food like plants do. Rather, they get their nutrients by digesting organic matter.

Fungi take many different forms. Some fungi, such as yeast, can only be seen with a microscope. These kinds of fungi live in colonies just like bacteria do. Most fungi are made up of thousands of threadlike cells that weave together

mushrooms

 form a visible fungus. They form
 reproductive structures that make
 pores, which are similar to seeds.
 Most fungi have spores that are small
 enough and light enough to drift on
 the wind for short distances. When
 spores land on organic matter, new
 fungi begin to grow from them.

ungus

Many kinds of fungi are good to eat or are used in the preparation of foods. Some are even used to make medicine. However, some fungi are poisonous and should not be eaten.

How Do Fungi Eat?

Fungi make and release enzymes that digest organic matter. Some feed o[n]
living organisms, but most feed on dead organic matter. Others pair up with
plants in a relationship that benefits both organisms. Most fungi are good at
breaking down wood and tough plant tissues. Shelf fungi are often found
growing on both dead and living trees.

BACTERIA

- one-celled

- live in colonies

- main decomposers of carrion

FUNGI

- most are made up of thousands of threadlike cells

- most are good at breaking down tough plant tissue[s]

- reproduce with spores

- decomposers

- found all over the world

- use enzymes to break down organic material

Mold

Have you ever left a piece of fruit on a table and forgotten about it for a long time? What did you discover when you finally found it? Yuck, mold! Mold starts when a spore lands on a piece of food. The spore begins to digest the food and grow larger. The spore spreads by producing rootlike threads inside and on top of the food. As the mold spreads, it also produces small structures that make more spores. In time the mold will completely digest the food. This breaks the food down into basic nutrients that return to the soil for use by other organisms. You've probably seen a moldy peach or a moldy piece of bread, but molds can be found almost everywhere in nature—even in water.

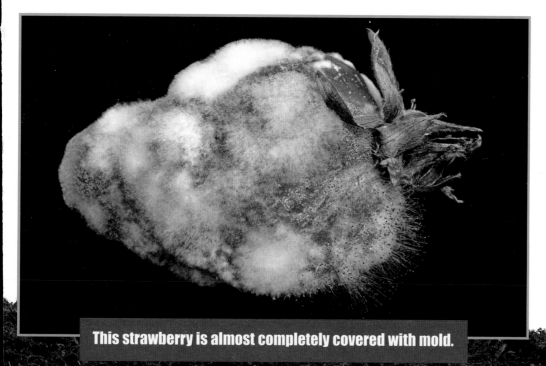

This strawberry is almost completely covered with mold.

Marine Decomposers

Underwater ecosystems are just like those on land. They have food webs made up of producers, consumers, and decomposers. **Marine** scavengers, such as crabs, turtles, and insects, break down dead plants and animals into smaller pieces. This creates plentiful detritus, which floats in the water where other smaller scavengers and detritivores can easily reach it.

Marine detritus eventually settles on the bottom of the ocean. Creatures that live and feed here are called bottom-feeders. Some bottom-feeders eat living plants and other bottom-feeders, but most organisms at this level are scavengers and detritivores.

Marine bacteria and fungi are the principal decomposers in marine ecosystems. Marine fungi often live close to the surface of the water. Some are land-based fungi whose spores fall into a body of water. Bacteria can survive everywhere in water. Some even survive around hot-water vents on the bottom of the ocean!

> Marine detritus is sometimes called marine snow because it slowly falls from the upper layers of the water into the lower levels, just as snow drifts from the clouds down to Earth. This turtle is creating marine snow, which will slowly drift down to bottom-feeders below it.

Composting

Remember the autumn leaves we talked about earlier? They're very important to life in a forest. As the leaves rot, they form a layer of nutrient-rich organic material on the forest floor called humus (HYOO-muhs). Forest plants get much of the nutrients they need for growth from this layer.

Humus forms naturally all over Earth. However, many gardeners and environmentally concerned people like to make their own humus. Man-made

umus is called compost, and the rocess of making it is called omposting. It's a cheap and easy ay to help your flowers and egetables grow big and healthy. 's also a great way to use your itchen scraps instead of throwing em away.

Compost is made by piling rganic matter into a bin or heap nd mixing it up as decomposers eak it down. Some people throw earthworms to help speed up e process. In 2 to 3 months, the composers break the mixture wn into humus, which can then used to **fertilize** gardens.

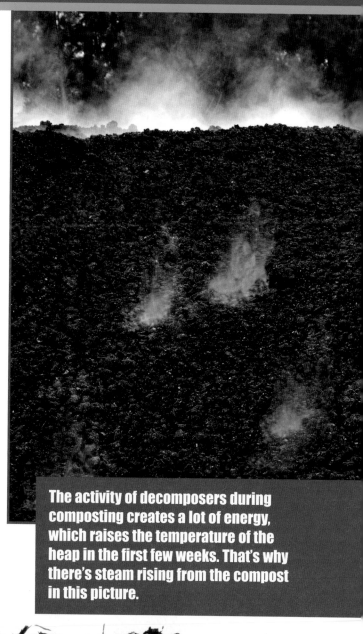

The activity of decomposers during composting creates a lot of energy, which raises the temperature of the heap in the first few weeks. That's why there's steam rising from the compost in this picture.

Let's Make Compost!

1. Pick a place for your compost heap or bin. It should be near water and in the open where decomposers can get plenty of sunlight and oxygen.

2. Start with a layer of "brown stuff": dead leaves and pine needles, newspaper, sawdust. Brown materials are high in carbon.

3. Add a layer of "green stuff": fresh lawn clippings, green leaves, vegetable scraps, coffee grounds. Green materials are high in nitrogen.

4. Mix the layers together a bit.

5. Add one or two shovels of soil. This adds decomposers—especially bacteria and fungi—to the mixture. It may also add insects and earthworms.

6. Add water. Keep the mixture damp, but not too wet.

7. Repeat steps 2 through 6 until your bin is full or your heap is large enough.

8. Periodically turn the mixture with a shovel and add water. This allows oxygen and water to reach all parts of the mixture.

9. After several months, the decomposers will have finished making compost. You can use the compost to feed your gardens and lawns while you start a fresh batch!

Glossary

carbon dioxide (KAHR-buhn dy-AHK-syd) A gas that plants need to make food.

carrion (KEHR-ee-uhn) Dead, rotting flesh.

chitin (KY-tuhn) A hard matter found in some plant tissue.

digest (dy-JEHST) To break down food so that the body can use it.

ecosystem (EE-koh-sihs-tuhm) A community of living things and the surroundings in which they live.

enzyme (EHN-zym) Matter made by cells that causes changes to other matter.

fertilize (FUHR-tuh-lyz) To encourage crop growth by adding something to the soil.

larvae (LAHR-vee) Insects in the early life stage that have a wormlike form. The singular is "larva" (LAHR-vuh).

marine (muh-REEN) Having to do with the sea.

nitrogen (NY-truh-juhn) A gas without taste, color, or smell that is found in the air.

nutrient (NOO-tree-uhnt) Food that a living thing needs to live and grow.

organic (or-GAA-nihk) Made from or having to do with plants or animals.

organism (OR-guh-nih-zuhm) A living thing.

protein (PROH-teen) An important element inside the cells of plants and animals.

reproduce (ree-pruh-DOOS) To produce more living things of the same kind.

spore (SPOHR) A special cell made by fungi and some plants that can grow into a new living thing.

survive (sur-VYV) To continue to exist.

tissue (TIH-shoo) Matter that forms the parts of living things.

Index

A
actinomycete(s), 18

B
bacteria, 16, 17, 18, 20, 21, 22, 24, 26, 30
bottom-feeders, 26

C
carbon, 11, 17, 30
carbon dioxide, 4, 17–18
carnivore(s), 5, 7
carrion, 12, 16, 24
compost(ing), 29, 30
consumer(s), 5, 7, 12, 20, 26

D
Darwin, Charles, 15
decomposition, 7, 8, 11, 12, 15, 16
detritivores, 12, 13, 14, 15, 26
detritus, 12, 13, 26

E
earthworms, 13, 15, 29, 30
ecosystem(s), 4, 7, 16, 17, 26
enzymes, 16, 24

F
food chains, 7
food web(s), 4, 5, 11, 26
fungi, 22, 23, 24, 26, 30

H
herbivore(s), 5, 7, 13
humus, 28, 29

M
mold(s), 22, 25

N
nitrogen, 11, 18, 20, 21, 30
nitrogen cycle, 20
nutrient(s), 4, 5, 7, 8, 9, 11, 14, 15, 16, 17, 20, 22, 25, 28

O
omnivore(s), 5, 7

P
primary consumer, 7
producer(s), 4, 5, 7, 26

R
rhizobia, 20, 21

S
saprotroph, 11
scavengers, 12, 14, 26
secondary consumer, 7
spore(s), 23, 24, 25, 26

T
tertiary consumer, 7

Due to the changing nature of Internet links, The Rosen Publishing Group, Inc., has developed an online list of Web sites related to the subject of this book. This site is updated regularly. Please use this link to access the list: http://www.rcbmlinks.com/rlr/decom